NOT WILLING THAT ANY SHOULD PERISH

Moreno Dal Bello

NOT WILLING THAT ANY SHOULD PERISH

One of the Scriptures most frequently used by those of the Arminian persuasion, when defending the unbiblical notion that Christ has died for every individual and that He wants everyone saved and none to perish for all eternity, is found in 2 Peter 3:9: ***"The Lord is not slack concerning His promise, as some men count slackness; but is long suffering to us-ward, not willing that any should perish, but that all should come to repentance."*** At first glance, this verse does appear to be saying that God does not want anyone at all to go to hell but that He wants everyone to come to repentance. However, only a superficial look at this verse would leave one with the impression that it is God's desire that *everyone* be saved and that none end up in the fires of hell. The promoters of such teaching say that, though God is willing that all be saved, none can be unless the individual makes that free-will decision for Christ to be their personal Savior and that the best, indeed most, that God can do for a person's salvation has been done and all He can do now is sit and hope that none will perish but that all shall come to repentance. In other words, what they teach is that it is not God and *His* will which makes the difference between saved and lost (1 Cor. 4:7), but the individual's acceptance of what Christ has done. One vital point that must be made at the outset of this study is: **what God desires never conflicts with what He causes to come to pass.** Those who have been taught nothing but Arminian doctrines, such as universal atonement and salvation by a 'free-will decision for Christ', have never been properly taught what this passage of Scripture in 2 Peter 3 is actually saying in light of its context and other Scriptures. Unlike those who fail, for whatever reason, to provide a proper biblical analysis of Scripture, this booklet shall provide the reader with an accurate, contextual examination of the verse in question and will also examine it in light of other Scriptures in order to see if what we teach that the Lord is saying here is in accord with the rest of His Word. The Arminian interpretation of this verse is a direct attack on the Sovereignty of God, that is, everything that happens God has willed to happen and it *always* comes to pass (occurs) in every precise detail **as He willed it.** It also opposes such essential Gospel doctrines as election and Christ's atonement, His death—what He did on the cross and for whom He did it. This booklet will show exactly what 2 Peter 3:9 is saying and by this prove to the reader that far from negating essential doctrines of the Gospel of grace, such as sovereignty and election, 2 Peter 3:9 **confirms them.**

      It would be foolhardy for anyone to pick up a letter not written to them and walk away thinking that every reference in that letter to *'you'* is speaking about them. If John wrote a letter to Jim, would it not plumb the depths of utter stupidity and ignorance for Joe to come along, read the letter, and presume that every *'you'* in the letter is referring to him! However silly this may sound, it is precisely what occurs when so many read 2 Peter 3 and presume that the *'us'* and *'any'* referred to in verse 9 is speaking of every individual ever born and that it is *they* whom God does not want to perish. The first thing we need to look at and confirm, if we are to be fair to ourselves and in order to arrive at a proper biblical understanding of what this verse is saying, is to ask ourselves **to whom is it written.** This will go a long way to finding out just who it is that God does not want to perish, and will leave the reader without room for doubt or uncertainty as to who it is Peter is referring to by his use of the word *'us'*. Open your Bibles and take a look at 2 Peter 3. Read verse 9 and then cast your eyes back to verse 1 and you will quickly discover to whom the letter has been specifically written and who is being spoken about in verse 9. Peter writes: **"This second epistle, BELOVED, I now write unto YOU..."** The term *beloved* here is a reference to fellow believers. Whenever *beloved* is used in the New Testament it is either referring to Christ as loved by God (see Matt. 3:17, 12:18, 17:5; Mk. 1:11, 9:7; Lk. 3:22, 9:35; 2 Pet. 1:17) or of believers (Rom. 1:7)—often as a form of address **"wherefore, my dearly beloved, flee from idolatry"** (1 Cor. 10:14). The term *'Dearly beloved'* is also used in Rom. 12:19; 2 Cor. 7:1, 12:19; Phil. 4:1; 2 Tim. 1:2; Phile. 1; 1 Pet. 2:11. In John's first Letter he refers to fellow believers as **"little children", "brethren", "beloved"** (see 1 Jn. 2:1,7,12). In 1 John 3:2 one quickly discovers who the *beloved* are: **"BELOVED, now ARE we THE SONS OF GOD..."** In the New Testament the term *beloved* is used when describing those who love the Lord, meaning faithful disciples or followers of the True God, or those loved by the person using the word *'beloved'* (see Eph. 6:24; Js. 1:12, 2:5). The term is *"Spoken only of Christians as united with God or with each other in the bonds of holy love"* (see 1 Cor. 15:58; Eph. 6:21; Phil. 4:1; Col. 4:7). The *beloved* of God are those chosen by Him to salvation (Rom. 1:7, 11:28; Eph. 5:1). The apostle Paul often used the term *beloved* when referring to those converted under his ministry (Rom. 16:5,8,9,12; 1 Cor. 4:17; 2 Tim. 1:2; cf. 1 Cor. 4:14, 10:14; Phil. 2:12). In fact, you'll find the term *beloved* in most books of the New Testament: Matthew, Mark, Luke, Acts, Romans, 1 & 2 Corinthians, Ephesians, Philippians, Colossians, 1 & 2 Thessalonians, 1 & 2 Timothy, Philemon, Hebrews, James, 1 & 2 Peter, 1 & 3 John, Jude and Revelation. If the reader is not convinced by this great weight of evidence concerning who the *beloved* are and that it is to them that Peter speaks in 2 Peter 3:9, then allow me to refer you back to 2 Peter chapter 1, to the beginning of Peter's letter, the very first verse, and you will find out to whom this letter of Peter's is addressed: **"Simon Peter, a servant and an apostle of Jesus Christ, TO THEM THAT HAVE OBTAINED LIKE PRECIOUS FAITH WITH US**

through the righteousness of God and our Savior Jesus Christ." This, without a shadow of a doubt, shows conclusively that Peter is writing to **believers,** saved people to whom he refers as *'beloved'* and whom he describes as **those who have received the same saving faith as he has received.** So it is made abundantly and irrefutably clear that whenever Peter, in his second letter, is referring to *'us', 'we', 'our', 'your', 'ye,'* etc., he is speaking of saved Christian people **beloved** of God.

Pertinent to our study is the very interesting 7th verse in 2 Peter 3 which tells of the judgement and perdition of ungodly men, and has great bearing on the reason the verses which follow it were written: ***"But the heavens and the earth, which are now, by the same word are kept in store, reserved unto fire against the day of judgement and perdition of ungodly men."*** The word *perdition* means *destruction, to destroy utterly.* "The idea is not extinction but ruin, loss, not of being, but of well-being." This verse is speaking about a group of men, ungodly men, who **will** utterly perish. It is saying that there is a day reserved for the destruction of the heavens and the earth, by fire, that will see men such as these judged and condemned to perish for all eternity. This is **God's will** written beforehand. The guilty will not escape His wrath and must be punished. It is God's will that they be punished for they are ungodly: ***"...The Lord God merciful and gracious....keeping mercy for thousands....will by no means clear the***

guilty..." (Ex. 34:6,7; cf. Num. 14:18). The Lord is merciful and He is gracious to thousands—those whom He has chosen—but as for the guilty, those who are set aside for judgement and perdition, there is *no* mercy and **it is God's will that they perish, be eternally punished.** Speaking to the brethren (1 Thess. 5:1, 4), to those who are all the children of light (v.5), Paul the apostle says: **"...God hath not appointed US to wrath, but to obtain salvation by our Lord Jesus Christ, Who died for US..."** (v. 9,10). This verse shows clearly that **Christ did not die for those who are appointed to wrath, but for those appointed to obtain salvation by Him.** Peter also shows that there is a difference between those who have been appointed to disobedience (1Pet.2:8), and those who are **"...a chosen generation...that ye should shew forth the praises of Him Who hath called you out of darkness into His marvellous Light"** (1 Pet. 2: 8). God is willing that the ungodly perish.

A study of the context of the third chapter in 2 Peter reveals that Peter is speaking of scoffers who shall come in the last days with mockery in their hearts saying, **"Where is the promise of His coming? For since the fathers fell asleep, all things continue as they were from the beginning of the creation"** (2 Pet. 3:4). Peter assures believers that the end shall come, that there will be judgement and that it *is* the will of the Father that all ungodly men perish (v.7). The two verses immediately following 2 Peter 3:7 sees Peter seeking to comfort and assure believers, to whom it has been established he is writing, that **they** are not among those who will perish. Peter explains in verses 8 & 9 that God is not slack (slow) concerning His promise that He will bring down fire and damnation upon the souls of the ungodly. Peter explains this by saying **"...<u>beloved</u>, be not ignorant of this one thing, that one day is with the Lord as a thousand years, and a thousand years as one day"** (2 Pet. 3:8). In other words, God does not operate in time as we know it. Our timetable is not His timetable and, unlike a promise made by a man which has not been fulfilled after many years and is discarded as 'hot air' or 'empty', God's promise that the end shall come and that all ungodly men will perish in His Wrath is as sure as the day it was made. Peter says in verse 9 that it is not slackness on the part of God that has seemingly delayed the end, but the reason it has not yet occurred is because He is longsuffering or patient towards **US** (the beloved)**. God is not slack or lazy, but rather He is patient and longsuffering towards His chosen people.** Once it is established who the *'us'* are in verse 9 one can easily understand what Peter is saying. We have shown the reader that the *'us'* here spoken of is in fact *believers.* Further evidence of this is the fact that Peter, in saying *'us'*, obviously includes himself in that group or number (see 2 Pet. 1:1). The following verse clearly demonstrates to what end the longsuffering of the Lord towards His people is all about: **"...the longsuffering of <u>our</u> Lord is SALVATION..."** (2 Pet. 3:15; cf. Rom.

2:4). 2 Peter 3:9 is in reality saying **'The Lord is not slow to act in regards to His promise about the end, as some men judge slackness; but He is longsuffering towards the believers (His chosen; His elect), not willing that any of these, His people, chosen to believe in His Son, should perish, but that all these chosen ones, those who have/will receive like precious faith with us, should come to repentance.'** The end not having come yet is not due to God's being slow to act to bring it about but it is because He is longsuffering towards those He has chosen, not willing that any of *them* perish before the end comes.

When speaking of God's desire and His will, one is dealing with the same thing. The two cannot be separated. Whatsoever God wills/desires, **that** is what He does and **that** is what takes place. Consider the following Scriptures which attest to this: *"But our God is in the heavens, HE HATH DONE WHATSOEVER HE HATH PLEASED"* (Psa.115:3). In light of this single Scripture alone one would be hard-pressed to convince anyone that, though God has done whatsoever He has pleased, not all that He pleases—wills to be done—is done or comes to pass. *"For I know that the Lord is great, and that our Lord is above all gods. WHATSOEVER THE LORD PLEASED, THAT DID HE in heaven, and in earth, in the seas, and all deep places"* (Psa.135:5,6). Whatsoever God wants to do, **He does!** God does whatever He wants to do. *"And all the inhabitants of the earth are reputed as*

nothing: and HE DOETH ACCORDING TO HIS WILL in the army of heaven, and among the inhabitants of the earth: and none can stay His hand, or say unto Him, What doest Thou?" (Dan.4:35). God does, He acts according to His will, so how can He *do* anything or desire anything that is not in accord with His will, and in turn His will not come to pass? **God does whatever He wants and whatever He wants He does. What happens is His will and His will is what happens.** Otherwise, He would be a God Whose will did not **always** take place and therefore it could not be said that He does **whatsoever** He wills. **There is no room for impotence in a Sovereign God.** He has a will, a plan, for everything He has created and everything He has created acts in accordance with His Sovereign Will. Listen to God Himself speak in Isaiah 46:9,10: ***"Remember the former things of old: for I am God, and there is none else; I am God, and there is none like Me, declaring the end from the beginning, and from ancient times the things that are not yet done, saying My counsel shall stand, and I WILL DO ALL MY PLEASURE."*** Every desire of God is fulfilled, **always**, for He is God and He does whatsoever He wants. **In a sense God's every desire, everything He wills, is His command, something He orders Himself to do, and He fulfills all that He wills for He is God! GOD WILLS WHAT HE DOES AND HE DOES WHAT HE WILLS.** The fact that He is God ensures that ALL He wills shall come to pass. No desire of

God's, nothing He wills, has ever or will ever be left unfulfilled. Everything, right down to the last minute detail, will occur for He has willed it. No leaf shall fall from a tree unless it is God's will. Speaking of sparrows, the Lord Jesus says: **"...and one of them shall not fall on the ground without your Father"** (Matt.10:29). *"God, your Father guides and directs its fall. It falls only with His permission, and where He chooses."* There is not even a hair on our heads which is not numbered by God (Matt.10:30). **Because God is Sovereign, it stands to biblical reason that if God willed that none at all should perish then all would be saved.** Seeing that it is obvious that not all are saved, it is clear that **those whom God is not willing should perish are those He has desired to save and not appoint to wrath.** All those who do/will believe are those who have been *appointed* to eternal life by God: **"...as many as were ordained to eternal life believed"** (Acts 13:48). God does not wait for a person to make a decision to accept Him and then ordain them to eternal life, but He has first ordained them and in time, His time, they will believe. **This being the case, how could it be that God would be not willing that** *any* **person should perish and yet not ordain all to eternal life?** The Bible teaches that it is not man's decision for God that saves him but the will of God alone: **"Of His own will begat He us with the Word of Truth..."** (Jas.1:18). The Lord says: **"...I will have mercy on whom I will have mercy, and I will have compassion on**

whom I will have compassion. So then it is not of him that willeth, nor of him that runneth, but of God that sheweth mercy....Therefore hath He mercy on whom He will have mercy, and whom He will He hardeneth" (Rom. 9:15,16,18). God is merciful and compassionate. He is longsuffering, or forbearing, towards His elect people because He is not willing that THEY should perish (2 Pet.3:9). There are only two groups of people: those to whom God is merciful and those to whom He is not; those whom He is willing should perish and those whom He is willing should not. This is proven by how God acts towards them. *"Longsuffering is that quality of self-restraint in the face of provocation which does not hastily retaliate or promptly punish; it is the opposite of anger, and is associated with mercy, and is used of God (Ex. 34:6; Rom. 2:4; 1 Pet. 3:20)."* God does not deal with His people, His elect ones, those He has chosen, with anger but with longsuffering which is coupled with mercy, love and compassion. However, ***"...God is angry with the wicked every day"*** (Psa. 7:11). The word *angry* as used in Psalm 7:11 means *'to foam at the mouth'* ie., *'to be enraged' 'abhor'* (have) *'indignation.'* But towards His people, His elect ones, those He has chosen to be compassionate towards, God is longsuffering and merciful. **God's dealings with the wicked are not in accord with the longsuffering He has towards His chosen people, but with punishment and anger.** This is further evidence that those spoken about in 2 Peter 3:9 could not possibly be every individual ever born, but specifically God's own people. While Romans 9:22 speaks about God enduring with **"...much longsuffering the vessels of wrath fitted to destruction",** it must be noted that His longsuffering towards them for a time is *not* coupled with His love and mercy in order to bring them to repentance, as it is with His chosen people (cf. Rom. 2:4). But the longer that God forbears with such ones the clearer it will become that they are deserving of His wrath, and ultimate destruction. God endures those vessels of wrath *"...that are fitted for destruction by their own sin and self-hardening"* with patience and longsuffering. The difference in God's purpose of longsuffering towards His chosen, as distinct from that purpose of and type of longsuffering towards those whom He has not chosen unto life, is shown in 1 Timothy 1:16. Paul writes: ***"...I obtained mercy, that in me first Jesus Christ might shew forth all longsuffering, for a pattern TO THEM which should hereafter BELIEVE ON HIM to life everlasting."*** In the vessels of wrath *"...God is willing to show His wrath. He will show that He hates sin"* **God wills that these should perish.** *"If it was proper to show His wrath, then it was proper for Him to be WILLING to do it. If it is right to do a thing, it is right to purpose or intend to do it. As sin is an evil of so great multitude, it is right for God to be <u>willing</u> to evince His displeasure against it. This displeasure, or wrath, it is proper that God should always be willing to show; nay, it would not be right for Him* *not to show it, for that would be the same thing as to be indifferent to it, or to approve it."*

Some may concede, *"Yes, the 'us' mentioned in 2 Peter 3:9 is talking about the elect of God but that does not mean that the 'any' in the same verse is referring to the same group of people."* It would be a case of extreme *eisegesis*—the interpretation of a biblical text using one's own ideas, in other words reading into a verse that which is not there—to say that because God is longsuffering to *us*, the elect, He is therefore not willing that any individual ever born perish. Such an 'argument' flies directly in the face of what the fundamental laws of grammar demand and is diametrically opposed to the context of the chapter where this verse is found. To say that the *'any'* are not the people referred to as *'us'* would make as much sense as a captain of a football team saying to his players, *"The coach is being patient with us because he doesn't want any football player in the whole world to play poorly and lose his place in the team."* **There is simply no logic present in such thinking.** It is, however, logical and proper, according to how the English language is written and is in accordance with other Scriptures, that this verse is saying that **because God is not willing that any He has chosen should perish He is therefore longsuffering and patient towards them as He was to the apostle Paul in 1 Tim. 1:16.** If God does not want a person to perish, Scripture tells us that He has appointed them to obtain salvation, loves them and is merciful unto them (1

Thess. 5:9,10; 2 Thess. 2:12-14), that He saves those whom He calls His sheep and none of them will ever perish (Jn. 10:27-29). He will not bring about the end of the world until all these are saved and come to repentance. **The end of the world and the day of judgement of ungodly men awaits the salvation of every one of those whom God is not willing should perish.** The connection is clearly made in 2 Peter 3:3-9. Paul the apostle was of like-mind with the Lord when he said ***"...I endure all things for THE ELECT'S SAKES, that THEY may also obtain the salvation which is in Christ Jesus with eternal glory"*** (2 Tim. 2:10). Paul endured all his sufferings *for the sake of the elect*, that he might continue to preach the Gospel in their hearing that *they* also obtain salvation. Paul makes it clear that **this was not done for the sake of all people but solely for the elect of God.** God is Almighty! This means that He can do, and more to the point **does** do, whatsoever He pleases. If this were not the case, then how would God be any different to mortal man in this regard? He would be like any one of us. He would have desires and preferences to what He would like to see happen but He would have little or no power to ensure that anything come to pass as He would like it to. This contrasts sharply with what the Scriptures we have quoted above say of the Sovereign God.

    Even with all this evidence there will still be those who simply cannot, or will not, believe that 2 Peter 3:9 is not saying what they have been taught it says and which they have believed for years. They have been taught that *'God is not willing that any should perish. He wants everyone saved and has provided a Savior to open the door to heaven. Its now up to us to walk through that door and be saved'.* This is what has been and continues to be preached in christendom, and what's worse, believed in by the multitude.

But there is further proof that this verse in 2 Peter is not saying what so many believe it to be saying and it is found in the very words of the Savior Himself, Christ Jesus. Turn to Matthew 18 and you will see something that I doubt has been preached very much at all from any pulpit. Jesus Christ is here speaking to His disciples. They have asked Him, **"...Who is the greatest in the kingdom of heaven?"** (Matt. 18:1). Christ responds by calling a little child unto Him and saying to His disciples, **"Verily I say unto you, Except ye be converted, and become as little children, ye shall not enter into the kingdom of heaven"** (Matt. 18:3). Jesus goes on in the next verse to explain what He means by *becoming as little children:* **"Whosoever therefore <u>shall humble himself</u> as this little child the same is greatest in the kingdom of heaven"** (Matt. 18:4). For many, all this passage shows is that Jesus loves little children and that they will see heaven. When Christ walked this earth, of course He was kind towards little children etc., but *small children* is not what He is speaking about here. **He has simply used a little child to illustrate the fact that if a person does not humble himself as a little child, is not converted and become**

like a child, he will not see the kingdom of heaven. One of the reasons He has done this is because *"Children are, to a great extent, destitute of ambition, pride and haughtiness. They are characteristically humble and teachable."* To become like little children is all about humility, to see ourselves as God sees us and not as more than we truly are in His sight. Christ is also *not* referring to little children—infants or toddlers—in this next verse, as so many who have never really looked at this verse have ignorantly concluded, but is in fact speaking about believers: **"But whoso shall offend one of these little ones WHICH BELIEVE IN ME, it were better for him that a millstone were hanged about his neck, and that he were drowned in the depth of the sea"** (Matt. 18:6). The *'little ones'* Christ speaks of here are those who believe in Him, who have humbled themselves as little ones—children, and been converted. We see clearly then that the *little ones* Christ makes reference to here in Matthew 18 are not the toddlers and infants of Israel, but those people who **believe in Him. He is speaking about saved, justified sinners.**

      Now to the verse that will send shock waves through those who maintain that when Peter says in 2 Peter 3:9 that God is not wanting **any** to perish, that the *'us'* and the *'any'* mentioned in that verse refers to human kind as a whole. It is found in Matthew 18:14: **"Even so it is NOT THE WILL OF YOUR FATHER which is in heaven, THAT ONE OF THESE LITTLE ONES should perish."** There it is for all to see. I have not made this verse up. I have not put words in my Lord's mouth. I have not gone to some perverted version of the Bible in a desperate attempt to find support for what I am saying. I have simply brought to the attention of the reader what Christ says in His Holy Word. **God is not willing that any BELIEVER should perish!!** This is perhaps the clearest definition of 2 Peter 3:9 in the Bible and comes from the mouth of the Lord Jesus Himself. *This is not reading into a passage what is simply not there.* This is not forcing or twisting the Scriptures to say what they are not saying. That is the realm of those preachers who dare to distort the Scriptures and avoid others so that their lies can be presented as God's Truth. The Scriptures say that such men **"...are unlearned and unstable...",** that they **"...wrest** (pervert) **the Scriptures, unto their own destruction"** (2 Pet. 3:16). Your Bible says exactly what my Bible says. Christ's own words are **"But whoso shall offend ONE OF THESE LITTLE ONES WHICH BELIEVE IN ME..."** (Matt. 18:6), and later **in the same chapter** identical language is used by Christ which was used by Peter in 2 Peter 3:9: **"...It is NOT THE WILL of your Father which is in heaven, that one of these little ones should PERISH"** (Matt. 18:14). It cannot be denied that, contextually, Christ is here speaking about those who believe in Him and that this all fits perfectly with what the apostle Peter was inspired by the Holy Spirit to write: **that it is not the will of God that any of His people should perish. IT IS OF A SURETY THAT IF**

SOMETHING IS NOT WHAT GOD WILLS, THEN IT SIMPLY WILL NOT HAPPEN! If God does not want it to happen, who would have the power to override what He wills and make it happen regardless?

It doesn't stop there! In Luke 12:32, Christ Jesus the Lord speaks with similar language to that which He used in Matthew 18, **"Fear not, LITTLE FLOCK; for it is your Father's GOOD PLEASURE** (WILL) **to give YOU the kingdom."** Here He is comforting, assuring, the *little flock* (His children, those who believe in Him) that it is not God's will for them to perish but that they should receive the Kingdom. In John 6:39,40 Jesus declares: **"And this is the Father's WILL which hath sent Me, that of all which He hath given Me I should lose nothing....And this is the WILL of Him that sent Me, that every one which seeth the Son, and believeth on Him, may have everlasting life..." That** is God's Will. **Only those whom the Father has given to the Son are they whom the Lord is not willing should perish!** Everyone that believes in His Son is of those whom the Lord is not willing should perish. It is the Father's will that none of those He has chosen and given (entrusted) to Christ should perish but that all these who believe on His name may have everlasting life! How can you entrust something to someone with the desire that harm may come to it? The whole purpose of entrusting a thing to someone is for its safekeeping. **What would have been the sense in God having chosen a people for salvation and that Christ**

His Son should die for them, **AND TO SAY THAT THEY WILL NEVER PERISH**, if after all this there was a possibility that it was His will for some of them to perish? That some of them would not come to repentance? Moreover, what sense would there have been in God not willing that any at all perish and yet not doing anything to ensure His will was fulfilled, which in this case would have been giving (entrusting) them to Christ? **This would contrast with how God functions and why He is God!** Further on in the Gospel of John, Christ speaks again of those who had been entrusted to His keeping. In John 17:12 He says: *"While I was with them in the world, I kept them in Thy name: those that Thou gavest Me I have kept, and none of them is lost, BUT THE SON OF PERDITION; that the Scripture might be fulfilled."* If it is Scripture that has been fulfilled, you can be assured that **God's WILL has been fulfilled.** Here we have a window into 2 Peter 3:7,9. Christ says that all those whom God has chosen to give unto Him He has safely kept and there is only one that is lost and that one is a son of **perdition!** He is not a saved one that has been plucked from His hand, but one who is among those who have been appointed to God's wrath. The only ones who will not be saved are those who will come under judgement and face perdition. These are not the ones whom God wills not to perish but like Judas, the son of perdition, they are to perish that the Scriptures—**God's Will**—might be fulfilled. Earlier in John 17:11 Jesus prays to the Father, not merely for those disciples who were with Him but also for those who would believe through their word (Jn. 17:20), that the Holy Father keep those He has given to Christ that they may be one together with the Father and the Son: **"...Holy Father, keep through Thine own name those whom Thou hast given Me, that they may be one as We are"** (cf. 1 Pet. 1:3-5). Jesus was not praying for every individual ever born. He was not praying for the world. Listen to what Jesus said: **"I pray for THEM: I pray not for the world, but FOR THEM WHICH THOU HAST GIVEN ME; for THEY are Thine"** (Jn. 17:9). Jesus Christ prays for those who are God's chosen people. Christ's interest, as is that of the Father's, is with the chosen ones, that THEY not perish but come to everlasting life. **How odd it would be for God not to be willing that any individual ever born perish, and yet Christ not even pray for them but exclusively for those whom the Father had given Him.**

Perhaps an even stranger scenario than Christ not praying for those whom the Father supposedly did not want to perish is found in the following verse: **"Woe unto thee Chorazin! Woe unto thee, Bethsaida! For if the mighty works, which were done in you, had been done in Tyre and Sidon, they would have repented long ago in sackcloth and ashes"** (Matt. 11:21). Here we see the situation, as described by the Lord Jesus, of the people from the towns of Tyre and Sidon who would have, if the mighty works of Christ had been performed in their midst, **all** repented and come to God. Now, what would you think of a God who, if the Arminian interpretation of 2 Peter 3:9 is correct, is not willing that any individual ever born perish but that all of humanity come to repentance, allowing the people of two entire towns to perish in their sins **knowing** that they would have all repented had He sent Christ to them to perform His miracles among them! **That is a god of evil my friends and not the true God of the Bible.** Many say, as a result of being taught so many lies about the glorious doctrines of election and of God's Absolute Sovereignty, that *'the God of election is an evil God and not a God of love'.* One must be very careful using such language. It is not a light thing to call the God of election, Who is also the God of love, evil. Not all have been chosen to salvation (Matt. 20:16), therefore not all have been given to Christ to have their sins atoned for, and therefore not all have been chosen to believe and not perish. Christ spoke to the multitudes in parables and, when asked by the disciples why, Jesus answered: **"Because it is given unto YOU to know the mysteries of the kingdom of heaven, but to them** (the multitudes) **it is not given"** (Matt. 13:11). Christ, speaking to lost Jews said, **"...ye believe not, because YE ARE NOT OF MY SHEEP....My sheep hear My voice, and I know them, and they follow me"** (Jn. 10:26,27).

    This short study should make it abundantly clear to any who are willing to see and who do not fear the truth, that God is not willing that any *believer*, any *He has chosen for salvation,* should perish but that all of *these* should come to repentance and be saved. What 2 Peter 3: 7, 8 and 9 shows is that the end has thus far not come, not because it is something that has been forgotten about by God or because He is unable to bring it to pass, but that the seeming delay, the enormous amount of time that has elapsed since the promise of the end was first made, is not due to anything other than **God's unwillingness to see any that He has chosen before time began, and for whom Christ died, perish before hearing and believing His glorious Gospel.** Christ says of His sheep, which are all those whom the Father has given unto Him and for whom Christ died, **"...I give unto THEM eternal life; AND THEY SHALL NEVER PERISH, neither shall any man pluck them out of My hand"** (Jn. 10:28). According to the Lord Jesus Christ, those who will never perish are those to whom He has given eternal life, ie., those whom it was the Father's will to give to Him. **Imagine God not wanting a person to perish and yet not entrusting that person to His Son, thus ensuring that person would never perish!** God, as the Shepherd of His sheep, seeks the lost ones until He finds them (Lk. 15:4,5). **"For thus saith the Lord God; Behold, I, even I, will both search MY sheep, and seek them out. As a shepherd seeketh out his flock in the day that he is among his sheep that are scattered; So will I seek out MY sheep, and WILL deliver them..."** (Ezek. 34:11,12). There are no other sheep but God's sheep. Mankind is separated into two categories: **the sheep and the goats.** Christ says that before Him *"...shall be gathered all nations: and He shall separate them one from another, as a shepherd divideth HIS <u>sheep</u> from the <u>goats:</u> and He shall set the sheep on His right hand, but the goats on the left. Then shall the King say unto them on His right hand, Come, ye blessed of My Father, inherit the kingdom prepared for YOU from the foundation of the world....Then shall He say also unto them on the left hand, Depart from Me, ye cursed, into everlasting fire, prepared for the Devil and his angels"* (Matt. 25:32-34, 41). The ones who are saved are all those whom the Father has blessed (v.34), His sheep, and the ones who are lost are those for whom Christ did not become a curse by hanging on the Tree (Gal. 3:13), the goats. **These are the ones who are cursed of God, showing that they never were His sheep, never were the wheat that He had planted** (Matt. 13:24-30, 15:13), **never were among those He had entrusted to His Son, whom He was not willing should perish.** The kingdom of heaven was not prepared for the goats, but for the sheep of God. The ones who will not perish are those to whom Christ gives eternal life. These are the same ones God has given to His Son, they are His sheep, and the reason they will never perish is **because God is not willing that they perish! Why else do you think He has given them to His Son and why would He not**

give any to His Son whom He was not willing should perish? God has decreed, He has declared by His very act of electing these precious ones to salvation, that they should not perish. **No other group of people fit into this category.** The Lord Jesus also makes clear the fact that none of the chosen will perish in the following verse: *"All that the Father giveth Me <u>SHALL</u> COME TO ME..."* (Jn. 6:37). The elect of God shall not perish for God is not willing that they should perish but that all come to Jesus His Son. Even the enemies of God know that none can resist His will (Dan. 4:35). *"..O Lord God of our fathers, art Thou not God in heaven? And rulest not Thou over all the kingdoms of the heathen? And in Thine hand is there not power and might, so that none is able to withstand Thee?* (2 Chron. 20:6; cf. Rom. 9:19). **The elect will all come to Him for they have been chosen not to perish but to receive eternal life.** All those whom the Father has given to His Son He in turn gives eternal life and thus these shall never perish, for they have **everlasting life.** *"Whosoever believeth in Him should not perish, but have eternal life"* (Jn. 3:15).

It is an essential doctrine and an integral part of God's Gospel Message that all those whom God has chosen shall come to Him and that none of these shall perish. The security of all those for whom Christ died is assured because God's Word says all these *shall* come to Him and none shall be lost. This is in perfect accord with the fact that God has chosen, from before the foundation of the world, a people to become His own people—a people who, unlike those who have been appointed unto His Wrath, will be saved by His grace through the Righteousness of Christ. Paul, writing to the church (called out ones) in Thessalonica said: **"For God hath not appointed US to wrath, but to obtain salvation by our Lord Jesus Christ, Who died for US..."** (1 Thess. 5:9,10). Christ has died for these special people of God's own choosing and all for whom He died shall never perish, they have not been appointed to God's wrath, for they have, through Him, been given eternal life. Christ has died for them, He has atoned for their sin, so how could any of these ever perish? **How then could it be that God wills not that anyone perish for whom Christ did not die?** If God wants everyone saved, why then did He not provide a Savior for all instead of exclusively for His sheep, His called out ones: **"Husbands, love your wives, even as Christ also loved the CHURCH and gave Himself FOR IT; that He might sanctify and cleanse IT..."** (Eph. 5:25,26). **It was God's will that Christ die, make an atonement, for all those whom He has called out of the world. Why do you think God has called them out of the world? Because He was not willing that any of THESE should perish!!** All these teachings give God the pre-eminence in salvation and all the glory to Him. They do not leave any room for man to boast. Salvation is the Lord's (Jonah 2:9), and whomsoever He wills to be saved receives, in due time, the gift of salvation and all those who receive the gift do so because of the will and purpose of God. **If it is by reason of God's will that any are saved, then it stands to biblical reason that all those whom He does not will to perish will never perish.** *"According as He hath chosen us in Him before the foundation of the world....Having predestinated us unto the adoption of children by Jesus Christ to Himself, ACCORDING TO THE GOOD PLEASURE OF HIS WILL to the praise of the glory of His grace..."* (Eph. 1:4-6; cf. Rom. 8:28-39). All those whom He has chosen He has also predestinated NOT to perish. God does whatsoever He wills and so whatever it is that God wills (wants) comes to pass and that which does not come to pass is clearly that which the Sovereign Lord has not willed. **God declares the end from the beginning, as Isaiah 46:10 says, not because He has some mystical power that enables Him to see into the future and accurately predict what will occur, but because He WILLS it to occur. He is the One Who declares what will occur and what will not.** That is Sovereignty my friend and if the one you worship is not completely Sovereign over all of creation, then you are worshipping a false god. If the Lord willed that no one at all should perish then all would be saved and Christ would have died for all. But just as not all those born in Israel are truly of the Israel of God (Rom.9:6), not all shall be saved for many have been appointed to damnation (1 Thess. 5:9; cf. 2 Pet. 2:12). This is something which is very difficult for many to accept. But if one reads the Scriptures and allows the Scriptures to interpret themselves rather than referring to their favorite author or preacher or denominational brethren they will see, by God's grace, that this is the true God. Simply read what God says of Himself and you will need only a short time to realise that He is All-Powerful and Absolutely Sovereign. **None of the elect shall perish for God is not willing that any of them should perish. What would have been the purpose of election if it were possible that those chosen/willed by God to salvation could also one day perish.** The elect have not been appointed to His wrath but to receive grace and mercy. Can you not see how all this falls perfectly into line with what is said in 2 Peter 3:9, and that what is said by Peter fits with the rest of God's Word?

My friend, the Gospel is THE issue. It is a life and death issue. These matters of Christ's death and who it is whom God is not willing should perish are not things that a person comes to know, even many years after being born again. They are things that form the nucleus of the Gospel message and are at the heart of what every saved person believes, and are heard and believed at the time of one's conversion. **Not believing in them shows that a person is either believing something which contradicts God's truth or shows that if they 'haven't made their minds up as to what they believe' they are in ignorance, darkness, which is what the** saved are brought out of in the first place. Either way they are not believing the Truth. **None can be born again and remain in ignorance and darkness as to what the Gospel is.** The Bible teaches that one cannot believe in the true Christ until **after** one has heard of Him and believed in Him: ***"In Whom*** (Christ) ***ye also trusted, AFTER that ye heard the Word of Truth, THE GOSPEL of your salvation: in Whom also AFTER that ye believed, ye were sealed with that Holy Spirit of promise"*** (Eph. 1:13). One cannot trust in Christ until *after* one has *heard* His Gospel, and none are sealed with that Holy Spirit of promise who have not *believed* that glorious Gospel wherein Christ and His Righteousness is revealed (Rom. 1:16,17).

The true Christian Faith is not a religion, nor is it primarily a lifestyle. True Christianity is all about a message—God's Message: the Gospel. This Gospel reveals the spiritual condition of man and God's way of salvation. Salvation is *deliverance*. It means *to be rescued or freed from a place of danger and brought to a place of safety*. It also means *to be preserved, to be kept*. **Salvation is God saving, or rescuing, a sinner from the eternal punishment due unto their sin and transferring them to a state of eternal safety and security.** Now, how does He do this?

Before we answer that we need to find out why salvation is necessary in the first place, we need to see what God says about the spiritual condition of man. In the Book of Genesis we see the account of Adam and Eve. God made Adam and Eve perfect, free of sin, and gave them a beautiful garden to live in and enjoy, with wonderful trees providing succulent fruits. Their life was one of tranquil days of love, happiness and contentment and of peace with God. God said they could eat from any tree in the Garden, but warned, **"...of the tree of the knowledge of good and evil, thou shalt not eat of it: for in the day that thou eatest thereof thou shalt surely die"** (Gen. 2:17). Death, previously unknown, would enter their lives—not merely physical death, but also *spiritual* death. Adam and Eve *did* eat of the forbidden fruit and death *did* enter their lives that very day, just as God had promised. Physically, they did not die immediately but the ageing process of decay and corruption, the breakdown of their physical bodies, did begin that day. However, they did *immediately* die spiritually. They were no longer acceptable to God for they had become sinners and were unclean in His sight. This *death*, both physical and spiritual, has passed on to every person ever since: **"Wherefore, as by one man sin entered into the world, and death by sin; and so death passed upon ALL men..."** (Rom. 5:12). This is because Adam, the first man, was made the representative of all mankind by God. As their representative, Adam's sin was imputed (charged) to them, his descendants, the entire human race: **"...by one man's disobedience many were made sinners..."** (Rom. 5:19). The fact that both you and I sin offers undeniable proof that we *are* sinners and shows that we come from the sin seed which began with Adam. Just as a grass seed will only produce grass, so too, the sin seed will only produce sinners.

Most people readily admit that they are not perfect but a source of comfort for many is that they see themselves as only *'minor'* sinners. Most people's assessment of themselves is, *'I am basically a good person. I know I'm not perfect but at least I'm not as bad as that person.'* They judge themselves by comparing themselves with others and according to *this* standard, they judge themselves to be basically good people. But the reality of the situation is that **we have all sinned against God**: **"For ALL have sinned, and come short of the glory of God"** (Rom. 3:23). Man has missed the mark, or target, and as far as registering points with God—man isn't even on the scoreboard! Man in his lost state is under the impression that if he does his best then God will accept him, for what more can a person do than his best? But God says **"...every man AT HIS BEST STATE is altogether vanity** (unsatisfactory)**"** (Psa. 39:5). The **best** a man can do to recommend himself to God falls far short of the perfection which God demands: **"...we are all as an unclean thing, and all our righteousnesses** (good deeds) *are as filthy rags;* **and we all do fade as a leaf; and our iniquities** (sins)**, like the wind, have taken us away"** (Isa. 64:6). Notice that this verse of Scripture is not talking about our *bad deeds* being unacceptable, but that our **very best deeds** are as *filthy rags* in the sight of the Holy God. This is because we are sinners and all we do is imperfect and, therefore, unacceptable to a Perfect God. When speaking to the most religious people of His day, Jesus told them **"...ye also outwardly appear righteous unto men, but within ye are full of hypocrisy and iniquity"** (Matt. 23:28). Man judges according to the *outward* appearance but God judges according to what is in man: **"...for the Lord seeth not as man seeth; for man looketh on the outward appearance, but the Lord looketh on the heart"** (1 Sam. 16:7), and at the core of every man is the sin seed. **"The heart is deceitful above all things, and desperately wicked: who can know it?"** (Jer. 17:9). No matter how 'good' a man can become, all his efforts fail to address the root problem: **his sin nature.** If I may use the following illustration, man trying to get to God by what he does is like a man who has one foot nailed to the floor. **No matter how much the man runs, all he can ever do is to go around in circles! He never gets anywhere because the root problem, the reason why he runs around in circles and never achieves anything, is not being addressed!** He must address the root problem, which in this case is that his foot is anchored to the floor. **The fact that we are sinners is that which condemns us and it is a fact which none of us can change.** Nothing we do or don't do or stop doing can alter our sinful nature one bit. **A rotten apple, no matter how fragrant its**

aroma may be, can never alter the fact that it is ROTTEN! And no one is going to accept a rotten apple to eat, no matter how fragrant it is! So too, God will never accept an imperfect and sinful man, no matter how many 'good things' he might do, because his good deeds can never do away with his rotten sinful state. Man's condition and the fact that he can do nothing to change his state before God, is highlighted by God Himself in this next verse: **"Can the Ethiopian change his skin, or the leopard his spots? Then may ye also do good, that are accustomed to do evil"** (Jer. 13:23). **"...verily every man AT HIS BEST state is altogether vanity"** (Psa. 39:5). **"...there is none that doeth good, no, not one"** (Rom. 3:12). Where there is imperfection there is sin and where there is sin there can never be perfection, and therefore **no grounds for acceptance with God.** Despite all of mans' enthusiastic religious efforts, God says **"...There is NONE righteous, no, not one: there is NONE that understandeth, there is NONE that seeketh after God. They are ALL gone out of the way, they are together become UNPROFITABLE; there is NONE that doeth good, no, NOT ONE"** (Rom. 3:10-12). Quite a predicament isn't it?

The standard by which we *are* to judge ourselves is the one that God has set: **perfection**—and if we are honest, we will admit that we are **im**perfect. The Lord Jesus says: **"...Thou shalt love the Lord thy God with all thy heart, and with all thy soul, and with all** *thy mind. This is the first and great commandment. And the second is like unto it, Thou shalt love thy neighbour as thyself. On these two commandments hang all the law..."* (Matt. 22:37-40). No one, not even the most religious person around, would dare say he has loved God *perfectly* or his fellow man as himself. **So we see then that, far from being guilty of only 'minor sins', we all stand guilty of the greatest sins.** Consequently, the concept of 'minor' sins is a false one for to break even *one* of God's laws is *to be* guilty of violating the law as a whole. Sinners cannot be saved by the Law of God for we have rendered it impossible that any of us should be justified and saved by the law for we have broken the law and thus exposed ourselves to the penalty of the law. *"For whosoever shall keep the whole Law, and yet offend in one point, he is guilty of all"* (Jas. 2:10). God has made clear to us the penalty for sin: *"For the wages of sin is death..."* (Rom. 6:23).

Society often gets into an uproar when a judge lets a criminal off with just a warning or hands down a light sentence. The judge that does this is perverting justice, he is not a *just* judge. **When someone commits a crime, they should pay the full penalty that the law requires.** While it is true that God is a God of love and mercy, it is of paramount importance to note that He is also a **Just** God, a Just Judge. God declares of Himself: *"...The Lord God, merciful and gracious, longsuffering, and abundant in* *goodness and truth, keeping mercy for thousands, forgiving iniquity and transgression and sin...WILL BY NO MEANS CLEAR THE GUILTY..."* (Ex. 34:6,7) and *"...there is no God else beside Me; a Just God and a Saviour..."* (Isa. 45:21). In order for God to be Just and at the same time Savior without perverting His justice, His law must be obeyed perfectly and His justice, which demands full payment for sin, must be satisfied. How could this be accomplished?

God the Father has sent God the Son, Jesus Christ, into the world. Jesus was conceived in the womb of a virgin by the agency of God the Holy Spirit and therefore did not carry within him the seed of sin. He did not descend from Adam and was, therefore, without sin and wholly acceptable to God. Just as Adam is a representative, so too is Christ. But while Adam is the representative of **all** mankind, Jesus Christ is the Representative of **all those God gave Him**—those whom God chose to save—through faith in His Gospel: *"...God hath from the beginning chosen you to salvation through sanctification of the Spirit and belief of the truth; whereunto He called you by our Gospel..."* (2 Thess. 2:13); *"As Thou* (the Father) *hast given Him* (the Son) *power over all flesh, that He* (the Son) *should give eternal life to as many as Thou* (the Father) *hast given Him"* (Jn. 17:3). Being chosen by God for salvation was not something that was to be earned or merited, it was not to be a reward, but was solely according to His Will: **"(God) *hath saved us, and called us with an holy calling, NOT ACCORDING TO OUR WORKS, but according to His own purpose and grace, which WAS GIVEN US in Christ Jesus BEFORE the world began*"** (2 Tim. 1:9); **"*...He has chosen us in Him before the foundation of the world...Having predestinated us unto the adoption of children by Jesus Christ to Himself, according to the good pleasure of His will*"** (Eph. 1:4,5). Faith, like everything else pertaining to salvation, is a gift given by God, it does not originate within ourselves: **"*For by grace* (unmerited favor) *are ye saved through faith; and that not of yourselves: it is the gift of God: Not of works, lest any man should boast*"** (Eph. 2:8,9), and this saving faith ALWAYS believes THE TRUE Gospel, never a false one (see 1 Thess. 2:13,14).

Jesus Christ is the Substitute of all those God chose to save, of all those whom the Father gave to Him whom He willed should not perish. As their Substitute, He lived the life of perfect obedience to God's law that none of them ever could, thus providing the obedience they needed to become right with God: **"*...by the obedience of ONE*** (Jesus) ***shall many*** (those He represented) ***be made righteous*"** (Rom. 5:19). As their Substitute, He died and was resurrected, thus paying the penalty in full for their sins: **"**(Jesus) ***was delivered for our*** (those whom He represented) ***offences, and was raised again for our*** (those whom He represented)

justification (acquittal)" (Rom. 4:25). Jesus blotted out **"the handwriting of ordinances that was against us** (those He represented)***...and took it out of the way, nailing it to His cross"*** (Col. 2:13,14). God's Word says that all the sins of those for whom Christ died were **transferred** to Him, and that His righteousness would be charged to them: ***"For He hath made Him* (Christ) *to be sin for us, Who knew no sin; that we might be made the righteousness of God in Him"*** (2 Cor. 5:21). All those for whom Christ was made sin are those who will never perish, for they have been made the righteousness of God in Him (see also Gal. 3:13). The imputation of Christ's righteousness is the only way that God can remain Just and at the same time be the Justifier of sinners: ***"To declare, I say, at this time HIS Righteousness: that He might be Just and the Justifier of him which believeth in Jesus"*** (Rom. 3:26). God's Law has been fully and perfectly obeyed by Christ and the resultant Righteousness charged to all those whom the Father gave Him. **There is no reason for them to perish for they have the Righteousness of Christ.** And, God's Justice has been fully satisfied by Christ's death on the cross for the sins of His people. To be truly saved, one should **EXPECT NOTHING MORE and ACCEPT NOTHING LESS than Christ's glorious Righteousness as that which is necessary to attain and maintain a state of salvation.**

The popular yet false belief that there are many religious paths one can travel but that all lead to the same God, is a lie from hell which continues to deceive people to this day. **How can one group, for instance, which teaches that Jesus is not God and another which teaches that Jesus is God both be right and leading people to the same God?** Once something like this is pointed out it becomes clear that all the different religions or faiths do not lead to the same God, for not only do they differ greatly in what they say about God and the way to salvation but they totally contradict each other. Just as there are many wrong answers that can be given to 2+2, there is only one correct answer. So too, there are many false gods and many false christs in religion's supermarket, but there is only ONE TRUE God, there is only ONE TRUE Christ, and what you believe about God and about Jesus Christ will show whether you believe in the True or in one of the many counterfeits which cannot save. God warns that many ***"...pray unto a god that CANNOT save"*** (Isa. 45:20). Only ONE road leads to God: ***"Jesus saith.., I am the Way, the Truth, and the Life: no man cometh unto the Father, but by Me"*** (Jn. 14:6). Religion, even that which *professes* to be 'christian', claims to know what it is that man can *do* to *'make up with God'*. But their teachings about salvation are false, for they all teach that **man must do something** in order to get saved and/or stay saved. **This is the identifying mark of religion's false gospel.** The word *religion* comes from the Latin word *religare* meaning *to tie up,* or *to bind.* Religion binds you to a system of laws and duties which must be obeyed if you are to see Heaven and if disobeyed will condemn you to Hell. **God declares in His Holy Word that man cannot do anything to get saved, that salvation is 100% God's work from start to finish and that no one is saved who believes contrary to this.** What better news could there possibly be for man than to learn that God, Who demands perfection, does not save sinners based on their *imperfect* efforts, but on the *perfect* obedience unto death (the righteousness) of Jesus Christ. The Bible does not say that obedience is not necessary, that one can simply believe in Christ and then live as one pleases. Obedience is *very* important in the life of a saved sinner, **but that obedience is not what saved him or keeps him saved!**

This is the Gospel that saves. It is God's Good News. Only those who believe the Gospel, which reveals **Christ's Righteousness alone** as that which saves sinners and keeps them saved, will enter into Heaven **with nothing to fear**. Those who do not believe this Gospel shall be damned – condemned to Hell forever (Mark 16:16), for no matter how many 'good deeds' they have performed **their sins remain charged to them. Those whom the Lord is not willing should perish, never will perish, for they have been provided with a Savior Whose Righteousness alone saves.** God has given them to Christ, He has committed and entrusted to the charge, or care, of Christ the Savior all those whom He is not willing should perish and they shall all be saved. **Just as the Father has given them to His Son, so too, He has given His Son as Savior to His chosen ones: THOSE WHOM HE IS NOT WILLING SHOULD PERISH!**

"For I am not ashamed of the Gospel of Christ: for it is the power of God unto salvation to everyone that believeth....for therein is the righteousness of God revealed..." (Romans 1:16,17).

Please Contact:

morenodalbello@yahoo.com.au

Please Visit:

www.godsonlygospel.com

Made in the USA
Monee, IL
03 May 2026

49437976R00024